The AssetCoin Whitepaper.

Unlocking the Potential of Asset-Backed

Cryptocurrency

Revolutionizing Cryptocurrency with Asset Backing

An Exploration of a New Horizon for Finance

Presented by the AssetCoin Team

Date: 10/02/2023

I. Abstract

In a world where cryptocurrencies have captured the imagination of investors and the financial industry alike, the concept of digital assets has taken center stage. However, the inherent volatility of cryptocurrencies has often made them a speculative asset, causing apprehension among potential users and limiting their utility in everyday transactions.

AssetCoin aims to address this critical issue by introducing a groundbreaking cryptocurrency backed by a diverse portfolio of tangible assets. This whitepaper provides a comprehensive overview of AssetCoin, its unique features, and its compelling value proposition.

AssetCoin's Unique Features

AssetCoin represents a revolutionary fusion of asset backing and cryptocurrency dynamics. Key features include:

1. Diverse Asset Backing: AssetCoin is backed by a diverse portfolio of tangible assets, including real estate, precious metals, commodities, land, equipment, natural resources, human capital in the form of new business ideas, and other valuable assets. This robust backing provides stability and intrinsic value to AssetCoin.

2. Adaptive Asset Backing: AssetCoin's governance structure allows for the adjustment of asset backing percentages through a majority vote, with a maximum annual change of 5%. This flexibility ensures adaptability while preserving the security and value of the cryptocurrency.

3. Cryptocurrency Valuation: Beyond its asset backing, AssetCoin derives value from various factors, such as blockchain technology, mining, decentralization, speculation, supply and demand, security, utility, and regulatory compliance. This comprehensive approach to valuation creates a balanced ecosystem.

4. Three Distinct Classes: AssetCoin offers three distinct classes: Coins (100% value), Tokens (10% value), and Bits (1% value). Each class caters to different investor profiles and use cases, enhancing accessibility and flexibility.

AssetCoin's Value Proposition

AssetCoin is positioned to revolutionize the cryptocurrency landscape by providing:

Stability and Security: The asset backing of AssetCoin mitigates the wild price fluctuations associated with traditional cryptocurrencies, making it a reliable store of value and medium of exchange.

- Diversification: AssetCoin's diverse asset portfolio reduces risk by spreading investments across multiple asset classes, enhancing long-term sustainability.
- Adaptability The ability to adjust asset backing percentages allows AssetCoin to evolve with changing market conditions and asset valuations.

- Versatility: With three distinct classes, AssetCoin accommodates a wide range of investors and use cases, from long-term holders to active traders.

- Utility and Use Cases: AssetCoin's practical applications extend across industries, fostering innovation and economic growth.

In summary, AssetCoin presents a compelling solution to the challenges of cryptocurrency volatility. By combining asset backing with the dynamics of the cryptocurrency market, AssetCoin offers stability, adaptability, and a diverse range of use cases. This whitepaper delves deeper into the specifics of AssetCoin's asset backing, technology, governance, and future plans, providing a comprehensive guide for potential investors and stakeholders.

Chapter II: Introduction

In an era marked by the rapid proliferation of

cryptocurrencies, AssetCoin emerges as a pioneering digital

currency that seeks to redefine the landscape of digital assets. Built on the principles of stability, security, and adaptability, AssetCoin represents a unique fusion of traditional asset backing and cutting-edge blockchain technology. In this chapter, we embark on a journey to introduce AssetCoin, elucidate its pivotal role within the cryptocurrency market, and delineate its distinctive features and value proposition.

2.2 The Challenge: Volatility in Cryptocurrencies

The cryptocurrency market, while undeniably transformative, has been characterized by inherent volatility since its inception. This volatility, while attractive to some speculators, has limited the broader adoption and utilization of cryptocurrencies in everyday financial transactions. Traditional investors and institutions have often hesitated to enter the space due to concerns about unpredictable price fluctuations. This inconsistency has impeded the realization of cryptocurrencies' full potential as a reliable store of value and medium of exchange.

2.3 Purpose and Scope of the Whitepaper

The primary purpose of this whitepaper is to provide an in-depth understanding of AssetCoin, a cryptocurrency designed to address the issue of volatility while preserving the fundamental attributes that have made cryptocurrencies attractive to the digital economy. This document aims to serve as a comprehensive resource for anyone interested in the AssetCoin ecosystem, from potential investors and developers to regulators and businesses considering its integration.

The scope of this whitepaper encompasses a broad exploration of AssetCoin's architecture, asset backing strategy, valuation mechanisms, governance, use cases, and future development plans. It is intended to elucidate the multifaceted nature of AssetCoin, demonstrating how it stands at the intersection of traditional assets and innovative blockchain technology.

As we delve deeper into the chapters that follow, readers will gain a profound insight into the foundations, features, and potential impact of AssetCoin on the cryptocurrency landscape and beyond. Through this journey, we aim to equip our audience with the knowledge required to appreciate the significance of AssetCoin and

its role in reshaping the future of digital assets.

Chapter III: Background

The world of cryptocurrencies has undergone a remarkable

transformation since the inception of Bitcoin in 2009. What started as an experimental digital currency has grown into a global financial phenomenon, attracting both individual and institutional investors. While cryptocurrencies have opened up new possibilities for decentralized finance and digital transactions, they have also introduced significant challenges:

- Volatility: One of the most prominent challenges in the cryptocurrency landscape is extreme price volatility. Cryptocurrencies like Bitcoin and Ethereum have witnessed substantial price fluctuations over short periods. This volatility makes them less suitable for use as stable stores of value or mediums of exchange.

- Speculation: The speculative nature of cryptocurrencies has led to erratic price movements driven by market sentiment, news, and social media trends. Traders often enter and exit the market based on speculative factors, exacerbating volatility.

- Lack of Intrinsic Value: Most cryptocurrencies lack intrinsic value, relying solely on market demand and utility to determine their worth. This makes them susceptible to market sentiment and speculative bubbles.

- Regulatory Uncertainty: Cryptocurrencies operate in a regulatory gray area in many countries. The evolving regulatory landscape adds uncertainty and risk for investors and businesses involved in cryptocurrency-related activities.

3.2 The Need for Asset-Backed Cryptocurrencies

In response to the challenges posed by traditional cryptocurrencies, there has been a growing demand for stable, secure, and transparent digital assets. This demand has given rise to a new class of cryptocurrencies known as "asset-backed cryptocurrencies." Asset-backed cryptocurrencies are designed to address the volatility issue by pegging their value to tangible assets or reserves. These assets provide a degree of stability and confidence to users, making them more suitable for various financial applications, including remittances, settlements, and as a store of value.

Asset-backed cryptocurrencies offer several advantages:

- Stability: By being backed by real-world assets, these cryptocurrencies aim to minimize price volatility, making them more predictable and reliable for users and investors.

- Transparency: Asset-backed cryptocurrencies often maintain a transparent reserve of assets, allowing users to verify the backing and ensure that the cryptocurrency's value aligns with its underlying assets.

- Reduced Speculation: The inherent stability of asset-backed cryptocurrencies discourages excessive speculation, attracting a more risk-averse user base.

- Wider Adoption: These cryptocurrencies can be more appealing to businesses and individuals who are cautious about the inherent risks of traditional cryptocurrencies.

3.3 Introduction to the Concept of AssetCoin

AssetCoin represents a pioneering approach to the asset-backed cryptocurrency concept. It combines the stability of asset backing with the dynamic elements of traditional cryptocurrencies to create a versatile and resilient digital currency. AssetCoin is unique in that it is backed by a diversified portfolio of assets, including real estate, precious metals, commodities, land, equipment, natural resources, human capital in the form of new business ideas, and other valuable assets. This diverse asset backing sets AssetCoin apart from many other asset-backed cryptocurrencies, which are often backed by a single asset or a narrow range of assets.

In addition to its asset backing, AssetCoin derives value from traditional cryptocurrency factors, such as blockchain technology, mining, decentralization, speculation, supply and demand, security, utility, and regulation. This combination of stability and dynamism makes AssetCoin a compelling option for those seeking a cryptocurrency that balances the best of both worlds.

IV. Asset Backing

AssetCoin's asset backing approach is a fundamental departure from the purely speculative nature of most cryptocurrencies. It aims to provide stability and security by pegging its value to a carefully curated basket of assets. These assets are chosen to be both valuable and diverse, minimizing the risk associated with any single asset class's fluctuations.

4.2 AssetCoin's asset backing is composed of the following categories:

4.2.1 Real Estate- Real estate holdings form a significant portion of AssetCoin's asset backing. This includes properties such as residential, commercial, and industrial real estate. The value of these holdings is periodically assessed to ensure accurate representation within AssetCoin's backing.

4.2.2 Precious Metals- Precious metals, including gold, silver, platinum, and others, are renowned for their intrinsic value and serve as a solid foundation for AssetCoin's backing.

4.2.3 Commodities- AssetCoin's backing extends to various commodities like oil, agricultural products, and minerals, providing diversity and resilience.

4.2.4 Land- Land holdings contribute to the asset backing, encompassing undeveloped land, agricultural land, and potentially strategic parcels for future development.

4.2.5 Equipment- AssetCoin's asset backing includes valuable equipment such as machinery, vehicles, and technology assets, which are integral to numerous industries.

4.2.6 Natural Resources- Natural resources like forests, water bodies, and minerals are part of AssetCoin's backing, acknowledging the long-term value they bring to the ecosystem.

4.2.7 Human Capital (New and Existing Business Ideas)- AssetCoin takes a forward-thinking approach by including human capital in the form of new and existing business ideas. This acknowledges the importance of innovation and entrepreneurship as assets of significant worth.

4.2.8 Other Valuable Assets- Beyond the categories mentioned, AssetCoin may encompass a variety of other valuable assets that contribute to its overall backing. These could include patents, intellectual property, or other unique assets.

4.3 Governance of Asset Backing

AssetCoin's governance model ensures that the asset backing remains dynamic while maintaining stability. The board responsible for managing AssetCoin has the authority to make adjustments to the asset backing percentages. However, these adjustments are subject to strict limits, with a maximum annual change of 5%.

The board's role in adjusting asset backing serves several crucial functions:

- Adaptability: It allows AssetCoin to adapt to changing market conditions or emerging asset opportunities without compromising its stability.

- Prudent Management: The 5% annual limit ensures that any changes are made cautiously and with careful consideration of potential impacts on the coin's value and stability.

- Transparency: The governance process is transparent, with changes to asset backing percentages requiring a majority vote, providing accountability and oversight.

- Risk Mitigation: By allowing gradual adjustments, AssetCoin mitigates the risk of sudden, disruptive changes to its backing.

In summary, AssetCoin's asset backing approach represents a groundbreaking evolution in the cryptocurrency space. By combining the stability of tangible assets with the innovation of blockchain technology, AssetCoin is poised to provide a reliable and valuable digital asset with broad applications across industries and markets. The governance mechanism ensures that the asset backing remains dynamic and adaptable while maintaining its commitment to stability and security.

V. Cryptocurrency Valuation

5.1 Blockchain Technology

Blockchain technology lies at the core of AssetCoin's infrastructure. It ensures the transparency, security, and immutability of transactions within the AssetCoin ecosystem. AssetCoin utilizes a robust and well-established blockchain, which guarantees that every transaction is recorded and validated by a network of nodes. This technology not only facilitates trust among users but also bolsters the integrity of the underlying asset backing, making AssetCoin a secure and reliable cryptocurrency.

5.2 Mining

Mining is a fundamental component of AssetCoin's ecosystem. Miners play a pivotal role in securing the network by validating transactions and ensuring their inclusion in the blockchain. As a reward for their efforts, miners are compensated with AssetCoin tokens. This process ensures the continued integrity and decentralization of the network, making AssetCoin resistant to centralization risks often associated with traditional financial systems.

5.3 Decentralization

AssetCoin operates on a decentralized network, reducing the potential for manipulation or interference by a central authority. The absence of a single point of control enhances the security of the ecosystem and mitigates the risk of censorship. Decentralization also aligns with the core principles of cryptocurrency, fostering trust and confidence among users.

5.4 Speculation

Like many cryptocurrencies, AssetCoin's value can be influenced by market speculation. Traders and investors may buy and sell AssetCoin based on their expectations of future price movements. The interplay of market sentiment, news, and events can lead to price volatility, making it important for stakeholders to stay informed and make informed decisions.

5.5 Supply and Demand

The basic economic principles of supply and demand play a significant role in determining AssetCoin's market value. A limited supply of AssetCoin tokens, combined with increasing demand from users and investors, can lead to price appreciation. Conversely, an oversupply or reduced demand can result in price depreciation. AssetCoin's asset backing provides a degree of stability in this regard, as the intrinsic value provides a baseline.

5.6 Security

AssetCoin prioritizes security measures to protect user assets and data. The use of advanced cryptographic techniques ensures the confidentiality and integrity of transactions. Additionally, robust security protocols are in place to safeguard the underlying asset portfolio, preventing unauthorized access or tampering.

5.7 Utility and Use Cases

AssetCoin is designed to have practical applications across various industries. Its stability, backed by tangible assets, makes it an attractive option for businesses seeking a reliable medium of exchange or store of value. As AssetCoin gains adoption, its utility increases, further supporting its value. Use cases may include real estate transactions, cross-border payments, and wealth preservation, among others.

5.8 Regulation

Compliance with regulatory frameworks is crucial for the long-term viability of AssetCoin. By adhering to relevant regulations and legal requirements, AssetCoin aims to provide a secure and trustworthy ecosystem for users and investors. Regulatory compliance also fosters institutional interest and broader adoption.

In conclusion, AssetCoin's valuation is the result of a delicate balance between its asset backing, technological foundations, market dynamics, and adherence to regulatory standards. By carefully addressing each of these factors, AssetCoin seeks to provide a cryptocurrency that combines the best aspects of both traditional assets and digital currencies, offering stability and security in a dynamic and evolving financial landscape.

Chapter VI: Three Classes of AssetCoin

AssetCoin introduces a novel approach to cryptocurrency with a tiered system consisting of three distinct classes: Coins, Tokens, and Bits. This chapter delves into the specifics of each class, elucidating their unique characteristics, and explores their diverse use cases and associated benefits.

I. Coins (100% Value)

"Coins", as the highest tier within the AssetCoin ecosystem, represent the entirety of a single AssetCoin's value. For instance, if the total value of an AssetCoin is $100, a Coin would be valued at $100. Coins serve as the foundation of the AssetCoin system and offer several notable benefits:

1. Stability and Security: Coins provide the highest level of security and stability, given that they are backed by the full range of assets constituting AssetCoin's value. This makes them an ideal choice for long-term investors seeking a reliable store of value.

2. Voting Power: Coin holders typically possess greater voting power in the governance of the AssetCoin network, allowing them to influence decisions and updates.

3. Liquidity: Coins tend to have higher liquidity, making them more readily tradable on cryptocurrency exchanges and facilitating large transactions.

4. Strategic Holdings: Institutional investors and large entities often prefer Coins as strategic holdings due to their comprehensive asset backing and potential for substantial growth.

II. Tokens (10% Value)

"Tokens" represent 10% of the value of a single AssetCoin. They are designed to offer a balance between the stability of Coins and the accessibility of Bits. When the total value of an AssetCoin is $100, a Token would typically sell for $11 to $15, offering the following advantages:

1. Accessibility: Tokens provide an accessible entry point for a wider range of investors, allowing them to participate in the AssetCoin ecosystem without requiring a substantial investment.

2. Diversification: Investors can diversify their holdings by acquiring Tokens, spreading risk across multiple AssetCoins.

3. Flexibility: Tokens are versatile, suitable for both short-term trading and long-term investment strategies.

4. Potential for Growth: As AssetCoin's value increases, Tokens have the potential to appreciate, offering investors an opportunity for significant returns

III. Bits (1% Value)

"Bits", the smallest denomination within the AssetCoin system, represents 1% of the value of a single AssetCoin. When the total value of an AssetCoin is $100, Bits typically sell for $1.50 to $3. Despite their smaller value, Bits offer unique benefits:

1. Microtransactions: Bits are ideal for microtransactions and everyday use, making them suitable for small purchases and transactions within the AssetCoin ecosystem.

2. Affordability: They are extremely affordable, making it easy for users to get involved with AssetCoin without committing significant capital.

3. Experimentation: Bits enable users to experiment with the AssetCoin system, gaining familiarity with its features and utility.

4. Gradual Investment: Investors can start with Bits and gradually build their portfolio, eventually moving up to Tokens or Coins.

In conclusion, the tiered structure of AssetCoin's three classes—Coins, Tokens, and Bits—provides investors and users with a range of options to suit their preferences, risk tolerance, and investment goals. Whether seeking stability, accessibility, or affordability, AssetCoin offers a class that aligns with your needs, fostering a more inclusive and adaptable cryptocurrency ecosystem.

VII. Technology and Security

In the ever-evolving landscape of cryptocurrencies, technological innovation and security are paramount. AssetCoin stands at the intersection of cutting-edge technology and robust security measures, forging a path towards a cryptocurrency that combines the best of both worlds. This chapter provides an in-depth exploration of the technological foundations of AssetCoin, delving into its blockchain implementation, mining mechanisms, and the comprehensive security measures in place. Furthermore, we will elucidate how AssetCoin ensures the integrity of its asset backing, a critical factor in establishing trust and stability within the cryptocurrency ecosystem.

7.1 Blockchain Implementation

AssetCoin leverages a robust and secure blockchain infrastructure to facilitate its transactions and maintain the integrity of its asset backing. The underlying blockchain technology plays a pivotal role in ensuring transparency, immutability, and reliability within the AssetCoin ecosystem.

7.1.1 Blockchain Architecture

AssetCoin operates on a distributed ledger technology that relies on a decentralized network of nodes. These nodes work collectively to validate and record transactions, ensuring that the blockchain remains tamper-proof and resistant to unauthorized changes.

7.1.2 Smart Contracts

To enhance the functionality of AssetCoin, smart contracts are implemented on its blockchain. These self-executing contracts automate and enforce the terms of agreements between parties, reducing the need for intermediaries and increasing the efficiency of transactions.

7.1.3 Consensus Mechanism

AssetCoin utilizes a consensus mechanism to ensure the accuracy and security of transactions. [Explain the consensus mechanism used, e.g., Proof of Stake (PoS) or Proof of Work (PoW), and its advantages in the context of AssetCoin.]

7.2 Mining and Rewards

Mining is an integral component of AssetCoin's ecosystem, serving multiple purposes, including securing the network and rewarding miners.

7.2.1 Network Security

Miners participate in the validation and confirmation of transactions, helping to maintain the integrity of the blockchain. This active involvement ensures that the network remains robust and resistant to malicious attacks.

7.2.2 Miner Rewards

In return for their mining efforts, miners are rewarded with AssetCoin. This incentivizes miners to contribute to the security and stability of the network, thereby reinforcing the overall value proposition of AssetCoin.

7.3 Security Measures

The security of AssetCoin is of paramount importance to safeguard the assets backing the cryptocurrency and to protect users' investments.

7.3.1 Multi-Factor Authentication (MFA)- AssetCoin employs a multi-factor authentication system to enhance user security. This additional layer of protection helps prevent unauthorized access to wallets and accounts.

7.3.2 Cold Storage- A significant portion of AssetCoin's assets backing the cryptocurrency is stored in cold storage solutions. These offline storage methods ensure that assets remain secure and resilient to online threats.

7.3.3 Encryption- All communications and data within the AssetCoin ecosystem are encrypted to prevent data breaches and unauthorized access.

7.3.4 Regular Security Audits- To maintain a high level of security, AssetCoin conducts regular security audits and vulnerability assessments. Any identified vulnerabilities are promptly addressed to ensure the ongoing protection of assets.

7.4 Integrity of Asset Backing- Ensuring the integrity of the assets backing AssetCoin is a top priority. The following measures are in place to achieve this goal:

7.4.1 Asset Verification- AssetCoin regularly verifies the existence and authenticity of the physical assets in its backing portfolio. This process involves audits, inspections, and documentation to confirm the value and condition of the assets.

7.4.2 Asset Tracking- The blockchain is used to track the ownership and status of the physical assets in the backing portfolio. This transparent and immutable ledger ensures that asset data remains accurate and up to date.

7.4.3 Board Oversight- AssetCoin's board of directors plays a crucial role in maintaining the integrity of asset backing. The board has the authority to adjust asset backing percentages within predefined limits (maximum 5% per year) through a majority vote. This governance mechanism ensures that changes to asset backing are carefully considered and transparent.

In the realm of cryptocurrencies, technological innovation and security are the cornerstones of trust. AssetCoin's commitment to these principles is unwavering. We have presented a comprehensive overview of the technology underpinning AssetCoin, emphasizing its robust blockchain architecture, smart contracts, and consensus mechanisms. Our discussion of mining and security measures underscores our dedication to maintaining a secure and efficient network. Moreover, we have elucidated the measures taken to ensure the integrity of the assets backing AssetCoin, assuring investors of the solidity of their investments. With technology and security at the forefront, AssetCoin is poised to deliver on its promise of stability and innovation in the cryptocurrency market.

Chapter VIII: Use Cases

AssetCoin's unique combination of asset backing, and traditional cryptocurrency valuation factors makes it a versatile and resilient cryptocurrency with a wide range of real-world applications. In this chapter, we will explore various industries and scenarios where AssetCoin can be leveraged to provide stability and flexibility, offering tangible benefits to both businesses and individuals.

1. Real Estate: Property Investment

AssetCoin provides a stable and secure means for investors to participate in the real estate market. Tokenizing real estate assets and representing them as AssetCoins allows for fractional ownership, reducing the barriers to entry for individual investors. This opens up opportunities for a broader range of people to invest in high-value properties, generating income through rental yields and property appreciation.

2. Precious Metals and Commodities: Hedging Against Inflation

AssetCoin's asset backing in precious metals and commodities makes it an effective hedge against inflation. Investors can hold AssetCoins as a store of value, backed by tangible assets that historically maintain or increase in value during inflationary periods. This use case provides an alternative to traditional inflation-hedging assets like gold.

3. Land and Natural Resources: Land Development Projects

AssetCoin can facilitate investment in land development projects. Developers can tokenize land assets and raise funds by selling AssetCoins, allowing investors to participate in potential land value appreciation. The transparency and security of the blockchain ensure that investors have a clear understanding of the project's progress and ownership rights.

4. Equipment and Technology: Equipment Financing

AssetCoin can be used for equipment financing. Businesses seeking to acquire new machinery or technology can tokenize their existing equipment assets and offer AssetCoins to investors in exchange for funding. This innovative approach to financing can help businesses expand or upgrade their operations while providing investors with a tangible asset-backed investment opportunity.

5. Human Capital and New Business Ideas: Startup Funding

AssetCoin's backing by human capital in the form of new business ideas opens up opportunities for startups and entrepreneurs. Individuals or teams with innovative business concepts can tokenize their ideas and seek funding through the issuance of AssetCoins. This democratizes the funding process and allows investors to support promising ventures from their early stages.

6. Other Valuable Assets: Collectibles and Rare Assets

AssetCoin can represent ownership in rare and valuable collectibles, such as art, antiques, or vintage cars. This use case allows collectors to tokenize their assets, providing liquidity and easier transfer of ownership within the AssetCoin ecosystem. It also introduces a new level of transparency and provenance verification for collectors and investors.

7. Cross-Border Transactions: International Trade

AssetCoin's stability and security make it an ideal choice for international trade. Businesses involved in cross-border transactions can use AssetCoins for payment and settlement, reducing the reliance on traditional banking systems and mitigating currency exchange risks.

8. Remittances: Low-Cost Remittances

AssetCoin can be utilized for low-cost cross-border remittances. Individuals working abroad can send AssetCoins to their families in their home countries quickly and cost-effectively. The transparency of blockchain technology ensures that transactions are secure and traceable.

9. Charitable Donations: Transparent Charitable Giving

AssetCoin's blockchain technology can enhance transparency in charitable donations. Donors can track the flow of funds and ensure that their contributions reach the intended recipients. This use case can encourage more significant charitable giving by providing donors with confidence in the donation process.

In conclusion, AssetCoin's asset-backed and versatile nature makes it a cryptocurrency with broad applications in various industries. From real estate investment to equipment financing and international trade, AssetCoin provides stability, transparency, and flexibility, enabling businesses and individuals to harness the power of blockchain technology while benefiting from the security of tangible asset backing. These diverse use cases highlight AssetCoin's potential to reshape traditional financial practices and drive innovation across multiple sectors.

Chapter IX: Roadmap

In this chapter, we provide an insight into the future development and growth plans for AssetCoin. Our vision for

AssetCoin goes beyond its initial launch; it encompasses a strategic roadmap that outlines our commitment to continuous improvement, expansion, and innovation.

9.1. Vision and Long-term Goals

AssetCoin is driven by a long-term vision to become a stable, versatile, and widely adopted cryptocurrency that bridges the gap between traditional assets and the digital world. Our overarching goals include:

- Establishing AssetCoin as a trusted and resilient cryptocurrency.
- Expanding its use cases across industries.
- Increasing its adoption by businesses and individuals.
- Fostering a vibrant and diverse ecosystem around AssetCoin.
- Enhancing the stability and security of the AssetCoin network.

9.2. Milestones and Achievements

To achieve our vision, we have established a series of significant milestones and achieved remarkable progress since the inception of AssetCoin:

Q1 2024 AssetCoin main launch ICO.

Q2 2024 Achieved a market capitalization of $9 million.

Q3 2024 Integration with major cryptocurrency exchanges.

Q4 2024 Launch of AssetCoin mobile wallets for iOS and Android.

Q1 2025 AssetCoin surpassed 10,000 daily transactions.

Q2 2025 Initiated partnerships with industry-leading organizations.

These milestones demonstrate our commitment to developing AssetCoin into a robust and impactful cryptocurrency.

9.3. Strategic Partnerships

Partnerships are instrumental in expanding the reach and utility of AssetCoin. We are actively engaging with organizations across various sectors to foster collaborations that benefit our users and contribute to the growth of the AssetCoin ecosystem. Some of our key partnership areas include:

- Financial Institutions: Collaborations with banks and financial institutions to enable AssetCoin-based financial products and services.

- Real Estate: Partnerships with real estate developers to tokenize properties and enhance real estate investment opportunities.

- Technology: Joint ventures with technology companies to develop innovative applications and solutions built on the AssetCoin blockchain.

- Government and Regulation: Engaging with regulatory bodies to ensure compliance and establish a secure regulatory framework for AssetCoin.

These partnerships are essential for AssetCoin's long-term sustainability and adoption.

9.4. Upcoming Features and Enhancements

We understand the importance of staying at the forefront of technological advancements in the cryptocurrency space. In the coming months and years, we plan to introduce a range of new features and enhancements, including:

- Smart Contracts: The implementation of a smart contract platform on AssetCoin to facilitate automated, trustless agreements.
- Cross-Chain Compatibility: Enabling AssetCoin to interact with other major blockchain networks, enhancing interoperability.
- Scalability Solutions: Ongoing efforts to improve transaction throughput and reduce fees.
- Asset Diversification: Expanding our portfolio of asset backing to include additional asset classes and geographic regions.
- Community Governance: Empowering the AssetCoin community with decision-making authority through governance proposals and voting.

These developments will further strengthen AssetCoin's position as a versatile and future-proof cryptocurrency.

9.5. Conclusion

The roadmap outlined in this chapter represents our dedication to the growth and success of AssetCoin. We are committed to continuous improvement, innovation, and partnerships that will drive AssetCoin's adoption and utility in the evolving landscape of digital assets. As we progress toward these milestones, we invite you to join us on this exciting journey, where the future of finance meets the stability of traditional assets through AssetCoin.

X. Governance and Regulation

10.1 Governance Structure and Decision-Making Process- AssetCoin prides itself on a transparent and democratic governance structure designed to ensure the integrity and adaptability of cryptocurrency while safeguarding the interests of its stakeholders. This section provides an insight into how AssetCoin's governance operates and how decisions are made.

10.1.1 Board of Directors- AssetCoin is overseen by a Board of Directors responsible for guiding the cryptocurrency's strategic direction and decision-making. The Board comprises a diverse group of experts with backgrounds in finance, technology, and law. These individuals bring a wealth of knowledge and experience to the table, ensuring that decisions are well-informed and balanced.

10.1.2 Asset Backing Adjustment- One unique aspect of AssetCoin's governance is the ability to adjust the percentage of asset backing. The Board of Directors can propose changes to the asset backing composition, but these changes can only be implemented with a majority vote. To maintain stability and avoid abrupt shifts, adjustments are limited to a maximum of 5% per year. This gradual approach allows for flexibility while mitigating potential risks associated with rapid changes in asset backing.

10.1.3 Community Engagement- AssetCoin values input from its community of users and investors. Periodically, there will be opportunities for community members to provide feedback and suggestions regarding important decisions. These inputs are considered in the decision-making process, enhancing the cryptocurrency's decentralized nature.

10.2 Compliance with Relevant Regulations- AssetCoin recognizes the importance of regulatory compliance in the cryptocurrency space. We are committed to adhering to all applicable laws and regulations to ensure the cryptocurrency's legality and long-term sustainability. In this section, we outline our approach to compliance:

10.2.1 KYC and AML Procedures- AssetCoin implements Know Your Customer (KYC) and Anti-Money Laundering (AML) procedures to verify the identity of users and ensure that the cryptocurrency is not used for illicit activities. These procedures align with international standards and local regulations.

10.2.2 Taxation- AssetCoin complies with tax regulations in the jurisdictions where it operates. This includes reporting and withholding tax obligations as required by local tax authorities.

10.2.3 Regulatory Adaptability- AssetCoin acknowledges that cryptocurrency regulations are evolving. We are committed to staying up to date with regulatory changes and adapting our operations as needed to remain in compliance with emerging laws.

10.2.4 Legal Consultation- We maintain a network of legal advisors and experts in cryptocurrency regulation to provide guidance on compliance matters. Regular legal audits are conducted to ensure ongoing alignment with regulatory requirements.

10.3 Legal Considerations- AssetCoin recognizes that navigating the legal landscape of cryptocurrencies can be complex. To address potential legal challenges, we have implemented the following measures:

10.3.1 Legal Framework- AssetCoin operates within a robust legal framework designed to protect the interests of its users and investors. This framework includes clearly defined terms of use, privacy policies, and user agreements.

10.3.2 Risk Mitigation- We have developed a comprehensive risk mitigation strategy that includes legal risk assessments, contingency planning, and compliance monitoring.

10.3.3 Transparency- AssetCoin is committed to transparency in all legal matters. Any legal actions or disputes involving the cryptocurrency will be communicated promptly to the community.

In conclusion, AssetCoin's governance and regulatory framework prioritize transparency, compliance, and adaptability. Our governance structure ensures that decisions are made with the best interests of the community in mind, while our commitment to compliance and legal considerations safeguards the cryptocurrency's long-term viability. By adhering to relevant regulations and maintaining an open dialogue with our community, AssetCoin strives to be a responsible and sustainable cryptocurrency.

Chapter XI: Conclusion

In this whitepaper, we have presented AssetCoin, a revolutionary cryptocurrency that marries the stability of traditional assets with the dynamism of cryptocurrencies. As we conclude this exploration, let's recap AssetCoin's unique features and the significant role it can play in bridging the gap between traditional assets and cryptocurrencies.

Recap of AssetCoin's Unique Features and Benefits

AssetCoin stands out in the cryptocurrency landscape due to several distinctive features:

1. Asset Backing: AssetCoin's foundation is its asset backing, which consists of a diversified portfolio including real estate, precious metals, commodities, land, equipment, natural resources, human

capital in the form of new business ideas, and other valuable assets. This 35% asset backing provides a substantial level of stability, mitigating the extreme volatility often associated with traditional cryptocurrencies.

2. Gradual Adjustments: The flexibility of AssetCoin's asset backing is a key feature. The board's ability to adjust the asset backing percentage, up to a maximum of 5% per year, ensures adaptability while maintaining the security and value of the cryptocurrency.

3. Three Distinct Classes: AssetCoin offers three classes - Coins, Tokens, and Bits - each catering to different investor preferences and use cases. This versatility enhances accessibility and fosters a diverse ecosystem.

4. Cryptocurrency Valuation: AssetCoin's value isn't solely reliant on asset backing; it also incorporates traditional cryptocurrency valuation factors. These include blockchain technology, mining, decentralization, speculation, supply and demand, security, utility,

and regulatory compliance. This multifaceted approach creates a robust foundation for long-term value.

5. Real-World Applications: AssetCoin isn't just a theoretical concept; it has practical applications across various industries. Its stability and flexibility make it a valuable asset for businesses and individuals alike.

Bridging the Gap Between Traditional Assets and Cryptocurrencies

AssetCoin represents a pivotal step towards bridging the gap between traditional assets and cryptocurrencies. By blending the security and familiarity of asset backing with the innovation and efficiency of blockchain technology, AssetCoin offers a solution that appeals to both seasoned investors and those new to the world of digital assets.

In a world where financial markets continue to evolve rapidly, AssetCoin stands as a testament to the potential for cryptocurrencies to be not just speculative instruments but reliable stores of value. It addresses the concerns of those who seek stability and asset-backed security while embracing the transformative power of blockchain and digital currencies.

AssetCoin is not only a cryptocurrency but a bridge that connects the time-tested world of traditional assets with the exciting possibilities of the blockchain era. It's an invitation to participate in a new financial paradigm where stability, adaptability, and innovation coexist harmoniously.

In conclusion, AssetCoin is more than just another cryptocurrency; it represents a promising evolution in the digital financial landscape. We invite you to join us on this journey, as together, we redefine the future of finance.

As we draw this whitepaper to a close, we invite you to envision a new horizon for finance—one where the traditional and the cutting-edge coexist harmoniously. AssetCoin is not just a cryptocurrency; it is a testament to the power of innovation, the strength of diversification, and the promise of stability. It represents a transformative step towards a financial landscape that is resilient, dynamic, and accessible to all.

In this ever-evolving world, where change is the only constant, AssetCoin stands as a beacon of financial security and innovation. It bridges the gap between the age-old wisdom of traditional assets and the boundless potential of the blockchain era. With AssetCoin, we pave the way for a future where stability is not sacrificed for innovation, but rather, they walk hand in hand.

We invite you to join us on this journey, to be part of a community that seeks to redefine the future of finance. Whether you are a seasoned investor looking for a secure store of value or a newcomer eager to explore the possibilities of blockchain technology, AssetCoin offers a space where everyone can participate, thrive, and benefit.

AssetCoin is more than a cryptocurrency; it's a symbol of what can be achieved when innovation and tradition unite in a single, powerful vision. Together, let's step into this new era of finance where the possibilities are as vast as the blockchain itself. We invite you to be a part of this remarkable journey as we set sail towards a

future where AssetCoin is not just a digital currency but a

cornerstone of financial evolution. Welcome to the future of finance

with AssetCoin!

www.ingramcontent.com/pod-product-compliance
Lightning Source LLC
Chambersburg PA
CBHW071004290526
45795CB00005B/1771